DUI
Blackjack:

The **Ultimate Advantage** in Beating Your DUI/OVI Charge

Steven R. Adams

NOTGUILTYADAMS
WE DEFEND YOU LIKE FAMILY

www.NotGuiltyAdams.com
8 West Ninth Street, Cincinnati, OH 45202 **I 513-929-9333** © 2020

Disclaimer

This book addresses the Ohio and Kentucky criminal law related to OVI/DUI. It describes many of the decision points faced by a driver who is stopped and has consumed, or is suspected of having consumed, alcohol, drugs, or another intoxicant. Materials in this publication are for informational purposes only and are not guaranteed to be correct, complete or current.

This book contains general information and is not legal advice. An attorney-client relationship is not, and cannot be, formed with The Law Offices of Steven R. Adams, LLC until an agent of the firm and you sign a completed Legal Services Agreement. Do not send any confidential information or documents through the Law Offices of Steven R. Adams website.

This book describes some prior results received by Steven R. Adams. But individual results vary based on the facts of each case, including the jurisdiction, venue, witnesses, injuries (if any), and many other factors. The results described herein, and the client testimonials provided, are not necessarily representative of the results obtained by all clients or their satisfaction with Mr. Adams' services.

Images courtesy of. Lisa F. Young/shutterstock.com; sirtravelalot/shutterstock.com; New Design Illustrations/shutterstock.com; Paul Biryukov/shutterstock.com; Big Foot Productions/shutterstock.com; John Roman Images/shutterstock.com; Pazargic Liviu/shutterstock.com; StudioLaMagica/shutterstock.com; Alexander Raths/shutterstock.com; LukaTDB/istock.com; ncognet0/istock.com; avid_creative/istock.com; dcdebs/istock.com; Image Source/istock.com; RobertCrum/istock.com; SanneBerg/istock.com; KLH49/istock.com; kali9/istock.com; IPGGutenbergUKLtd/istock.com; LordHenriVoton/istock.com; aijohn784/istock.com; and johnnyscriv/istock.com

Book design by Graphique Designs, LLC

Printed in the United States of America

I THOUGHT YOU PRESENTED ONE OF THE MOST DETAILED AND FINEST COURTROOM PERFORMANCES THAT I HAVE SEEN IN A HEARING.

You did an absolute superb job from the standpoint of trial practice, attention to detail, argument. It was just an excellent presentation.

And I think that — and you have a lot of experience, and I think that kind of thing can have a tendency perhaps to overwhelm someone with less experience, but you were terrific. You handled yourself very well in the context of a skilled and thoughtful defense counsel.

– Judge, Hamilton County Municipal Court, statement on the record after motion to suppress hearing. Case no: C/17/TRC/15539

Contents

Introduction 1

1 DUI/OVI Blackjack! 3

  Initial "Observational" and "Personal "Contact" Evidence 4

  Pre-Exit Po Po Techniques & Exit Evidence 6

  "Standardized" Field Sobriety Test (SFST) Evidence 7

  Breath, Blood & Urine (Po Po Pee Pee) Tests 9

  You Can Control Your Cards—the Evidence Available
  to the Po Po DUI Dealer! 10

  Top Ten Do's and Don'ts for DUI/OVI Suspects 11

2 The Risky Ace Gamble: Breath, Blood
   And Urine Tests 13

  Breath Test Flaws 14

  Urine (Po Po Pee Pee) Test Flaws 15

  Blood Test Flaws 16

  Chemical Test Refusal 17

3 Face & Ten Cards: "Standardized" Field
   Sobriety Tests (SFST's) 21

  Horizontal Gaze Nystagmus Test; Walk and Turn Test;
  One Leg Stand Test 22

  NHTSA Final Validation Study: Revealing Quotes
  About SFST Reliability! 26

HGN-Medical Doctor Test-Not a Po Po Test! 27

Walk & Turn False Positives 29

One Leg Stand False Positives 29

Substantial Compliance Rather Than
Strict Compliance? Come On Ohio! 30

Non-Standardized Po Po Techniques 31

NHTSA Warning Label: "Validity May Be Compromised." 32

5 Reasons to Choose to Refuse All Field Tests........................33

Government Junk Science! 36

4   The Po Po DUI Dealer's Hand...39

Traffic and Equipment Violations: 2 or 3 Card 40

"Personal Contact" Evidence 42

Subjective "Odor," "Bloodshot Eyes" & "Slurred Speech": 4 Card ..43

Admissions: 5-6 Card..45

Extra-Ordinary and Unusual Actions:
7, 8 or 9 Card..46

5   3 Wild Cards for the Dui Blackjack
     Suspect/Player...49

6   Government's Burden: Proof Beyond
     a Reasonable Doubt...53

Ohio Definition..54

Kentucky Definition 54

7   DUI/OVI: A Crime Of "Opinion" 57

Under the Influence in Ohio 59

Under the influence in Kentucky 59

8   DUI Blackjack in Action 63

State v. J.D. 64

State v. L.S. 66

State v. R.S. 68

Conclusion 71

Appendix A: Ohio OVI/DUI Penalty Charts 73

Appendix B: Kentucky DUI Penalty Charts 85

Not Guilty Adams Contact Information 93

Author Bio 95

Accolades for Steve Adams 99

Introduction

Blackjack is a gambling game of chance. It is the most widely played casino gambling game in the world. One reason for Blackjack's popularity is that a skilled or knowledgeable player can increase his chance of winning. Nevertheless, the house always has the advantage under fair conditions with a fresh shuffle. A second reason for the popularity of Blackjack is its seeming simplicity. In this game, each player competes against the dealer to get closest to 21 without going bust (getting over 21). A player is dealt two cards, then chooses whether to stand on those cards or take additional cards. A player who takes an additional card is said to "take a hit." Each additional card carries the risk of "going bust."

As we all know, one advantage of the house (casino dealer) in Blackjack is that the dealer plays last. That gives the player every opportunity to make a bad decision or bust. You must beat the dealer to win but there is really no obligation for the dealer to beat you.

The dealer is dealt two cards, one up that is exposed, and one down that is hidden. Certainly, if the dealer's exposed card is an ace, a face card, or a ten, he has an increased advantage in winning. Unless you are an expert, or even if you are an expert in playing blackjack, you are still at a distinct disadvantage. Why? Blackjack is a game of chance. You win by luck. Especially over the long haul of playing the game.

Having said that, let's apply the casino game of Blackjack to playing DUI Blackjack.

FIRST, DO NOT DRINK AND THEN DRIVE. While it is legal to drink and then drive as long as you are not "under the influence" of alcohol and/or drugs of abuse, **WHY RISK IT?**

Take Uber, take Lyft, get a designated driver. Even for an unimpaired driver, being stopped for suspicion of DUI is a game of chance. By that I mean there are many people driving late at night who have come from parties, restaurants or bars, etc., and there are police officers out trolling for DUIs. Those police officers are planning on making DUI/OVI arrests for those folks driving late at night.

As such, if you have been out, and you have been drinking, taking prescription medication, or even ingesting illicit drugs, pay attention to the following rules of DUI Blackjack!

DUI/OVI Blackjack!

In DUI Blackjack, the dealer is the police officer a.k.a. the Po Po DUI dealer. The driver who is stopped by the police is the "player." In casino Blackjack, the dealer wins if the player busts, that is, takes too many cards and reaches a total greater than 21. In DUI Blackjack, the Po Po DUI dealer's chance of winning increases as the driver provides additional evidence and risks "going bust." In DUI Blackjack, "going bust" is a conviction for DUI/OVI. **WHEN THE PO PO DUI DEALER ASKS THE DRIVER TO SUBMIT TO A ROADSIDE TEST OR A CHEMICAL TEST, HE IS ASKING THE DRIVER TO "TAKE A HIT."** A driver who "hits" and is dealt a high card is more likely to bust.

The Po Po DUI dealer does have an advantage because he is trained to get evidence. He is trained to know how to stop and arrest citizens. He has nothing to lose. Moreover, through years of training and experience, the Po Po DUI dealer is skilled at manipulating and psychologically coercing people into providing evidence by getting the Driver to "take a hit", such as submitting to a roadside test or admitting to drinking alcohol. Collecting evidence is how the government attempts to win their case. The driver or "player" overtakes the Po Po DUI dealer's advantage by not providing evidence for the Po Po DUI dealer to collect. The DUI Blackjack player **GAINS AN ADVANTAGE** in beating the DUI/OVI charge by **NOT GIVING OR VOLUNTEERING EVIDENCE** (cards) like the following: **ADMISSIONS OF DRINKING**; in car or roadside field sobriety tests; and chemical tests (breath, blood, or urine).

The following discusses in more detail the strategy behind DUI Blackjack, and the various types of evidence the Po Po DUI dealer will attempt to "deal" to the driver to "bust" his hand.

Initial "Observational" And "Personal "Contact" Evidence

Evidence, in the game of DUI Blackjack, consists of the officer allegedly seeing you driving and committing a traffic violation or perhaps observing an equipment violation.

In addition, officers attempt to obtain observational evidence such as an **ODOR OF ALCOHOL, THE SMELL OF MARIJUANA, WATERY BLOODSHOT EYES, SLURRED SPEECH, ETC.** Also, the officers investigate and ask questions like: Have you been drinking tonight? **HOW MUCH HAVE YOU HAD TO DRINK?** Where are you coming from tonight? Have you been smoking marijuana? When the officer asks you these questions, **HE IS ASKING YOU TO "TAKE A HIT."** If you, the DUI Blackjack player, admit and say yes to one of those questions, you have effectively taken a hit and received a big card toward busting. You have given the Po Po DUI dealer a bigger advantage by giving him evidence. Even if you reply that you have not been drinking, if the officer notes an odor of alcohol, you have still "taken a hit" and offered evidence. **CHOOSE TO REFUSE TO ANSWER** the Po Po DUI dealer's questions. Just say: **"OFFICER, BEFORE I SAY OR DO ANYTHING, I WANT TO TALK TO ATTORNEY STEVEN R. ADAMS."** ▪ ▬ ▬ ▬ ▬ ▬ ▬ ▬ ▬ ▬

In doing so, be polite and respectful to avoid giving evidence in the form of belligerent or argumentative behavior.

[STEVE] IS OUT TO PROTECT HIS CLIENTS AND PUT THEM AT EASE! This is my first experience with an attorney. He was recommended by a Law Enforcement Officer. Can there be a better endorsement than that? He took all of the facts during a meeting with me. He made me feel at ease and that the situation would be handled well, professionally, and that my huge mistake would be in my past.

> **"STEVE'S OPENING AND CLOSING WERE AMAZING**, and I could tell the jury was impressed. Thanks to Steve and everyone at his office, the jury found me **NOT GUILTY** of DUI."

Pre-Exit Po Po Techniques & Exit Evidence

Next, the Po Po DUI dealer may attempt to collect evidence by asking you to perform **NON-STANDARDIZED PSYCHO-MOTOR TECHNIQUES SUCH AS (A MODIFIED VERSION OF THE ALPHABET, COUNTING BACKWARDS, AND A FINGER COUNT DEXTERITY EXAMINATION).** These are referred to as pre-exit techniques because they are frequently done before the driver is asked to exit the vehicle. If you are the DUI Blackjack player, and you agree to perform these techniques, **YOU ARE RISKING TAKING ANOTHER HIT TOWARD A BUST,** by giving the Po Po DUI dealer additional evidence and even more of an advantage. Choose to Refuse to give the Po Po DUI dealer pre-exit technique evidence. Instead say: **"OFFICER, BEFORE I SAY OR DO ANYTHING, I WANT TO TALK TO ATTORNEY STEVEN R. ADAMS."**

"Standardized" Field Sobriety Test (SFST) Evidence

The Po Po DUI Dealer will then request that you exit your vehicle to do some roadside "standardized" field sobriety tests like the Horizontal Gaze Nystagmus Test; Walk and Turn Test; and One Leg Stand Test. **DO EXIT YOUR CAR. HOWEVER, DO NOT AGREE TO SUBMIT TO THE ROADSIDE FIELD SOBRIETY TESTS. THEY ARE VOLUNTARY.** You do not have to do them. These tests risk a very big hit toward a bust —DUI conviction. So do not perform these tests! Once again, politely say: "OFFICER, BEFORE I SAY OR DO ANYTHING, I WANT TO TALK TO ATTORNEY STEVEN R. ADAMS."

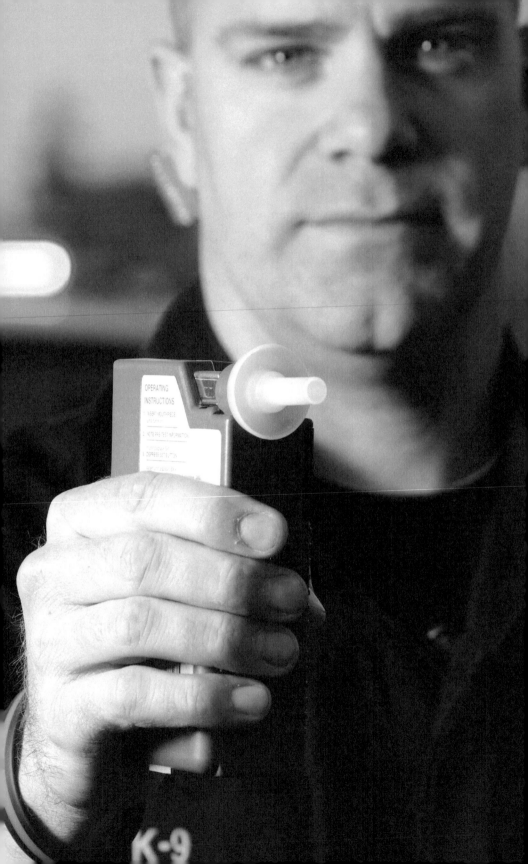

OPERATING
INSTRUCTIONS

K-9

Breath, Blood & Urine (Po Po Pee Pee) Tests

The Po Po DUI dealer may offer you a portable breath test at the scene and later offer you an evidential breath test or urine test at a police station. If you are involved in an accident he will ask for a blood test at the hospital. By consenting you are giving them more opportunities to collect evidence to find out whether you are under or over the Illegal limit of 0.08 blood alcohol content. You may even have amounts of prescription medication or illicit drugs in your urine or blood that they will want to use against you.

As it relates to a request for you to take a **PORTABLE BREATH TEST (PBT) AT THE SCENE, DO NOT DO IT!** Portable breath test BAC numerical results are not admissible at trial in Ohio and Kentucky, because the courts have not found them to be reliable evidentiary breath test machines. Furthermore, the police officer does not have to show you, or tell you, about the PBT result. So do not take that test. Choose to refuse to give the Po Po DUI dealer that type of police junk science evidence. Once again say: "OFFICER, BEFORE I SAY OR DO ANYTHING, I WANT TO TALK TO ATTORNEY STEVEN R. ADAMS."

> If you make the decision to hire Steve Adams, expect to be represented by an **INTELLIGENT, WELL PREPARED, BULLDOG.**

Also, make sure you also **CHOOSE TO REFUSE ANY BREATH, BLOOD, AND/OR URINE TESTS** that the police will request that you take after your arrest. These are evidentiary tests, and a test over the limit can be a very damaging card in DUI Blackjack. **DO NOT GIVE THEM THAT EVIDENCE!** CHOOSE TO REFUSE!

So now that we know that you chose to refuse and said, "No No to the Po Po," it is betting time. You may get arrested. But feel good about the odds of prevailing in this game of DUI Blackjack.

You Can Control Your Cards— the Evidence Available to the Po Po DUI Dealer!

In essence, the Po Po DUI dealer has an advantage in prevailing should you (the player) take hits by offering evidence leading to a "bust." The more evidence you provide, the greater the advantage for the Po Po DUI dealer. The less evidence you provide to the Po Po DUI dealer, the greater advantage that you have in either getting your case dismissed for lack of probable cause or winning at trial; i.e. **A NOT GUILTY FINDING!**

Top Ten Do's And Don'ts For DUI/OVI Suspects

1. **DO** retrieve your license, registration, and insurance before the officer approaches, if possible. Produce them upon request.

2. **DO NOT** answer questions about where or what you have been drinking. Tell the officer, "I want to speak to an attorney before I say or do anything."

3. **DO** get out of your vehicle if asked to do so by the officer.

4. **DO NOT** submit to any roadside sobriety tests, agility tests, or eye tests. All of these tests are voluntary, highly subjective, and are designed to incriminate you. Tell the officer, "I want to speak to an attorney before I say or do anything."

5. **DO** be polite without giving the officer any evidence. Make the government prove their case without your help.

6. **DO NOT** consent to a search of your vehicle.

7. **DO** remember you have a right to remain silent.

8. **DO NOT** take any tests that the officer requests of your breath, blood or urine until and/or unless you consult with an attorney.

9. **DO** remember you have the right to appeal any license suspension imposed upon you for refusing to take these tests.

10. **DO NOT** get pressured into submitting to field sobriety tests or chemical tests. These scientifically unreliable tests will not help you.

The Risky Ace Gamble: Breath, Blood And Urine Tests

2

In the game of DUI Blackjack, when the Po Po DUI dealer is "dealing cards," he will ask you to submit to a chemical test. The chemical test is a very risky card. **ONLY IF YOU ABSOLUTELY KNOW THAT YOU HAVE NO ALCOHOL OR DRUGS IN YOUR SYSTEM, SHOULD YOU CONSIDER TAKING A CHEMICAL TEST.** A positive chemical test is like giving an Ace to the State. Note that drugs such as marijuana can remain detectable for over 90 days. A chemical test at or above the legal limit gives the State very strong evidence toward a conviction. You do not want to take this hit and give the Po Po DUI dealer an Ace card. A chemical test is a breath test, urine test (Po Po pee pee test), or a blood test. The Po Po DUI dealer chooses which test and can ask you to submit to more than of these chemical tests.

Chemical testing, has an aura of "science" and "reliability" yet these tests can be flawed.

Breath Test Flaws

The government claims that the breath test machine is "scientific," but the truth is that **BREATH TESTING IS VERY UNRELIABLE AND INACCURATE.** There are machine based flaws, such as...

✓   lack of concurrent calibration checks;

✓   no warranty;

✓   lack of computerized online breath archives;

✓   there is an inherent margin of error with these machines;

✓   and radio frequency interference.

Also, there are operator errors that can cause unreliable and inaccurate results such as...

✓   inadequate mouth alcohol deprivation-which accounts for residual mouth alcohol;

✓   improper breath testing instructions making the suspect blow excessively long ("the more you blow the higher you go");

✓   forced agreement where the breath test operator interrupts the subjects breathing pattern forcing agreement of the two samples.

Moreover, the subject taking the breath test may have physiological issues that can cause the machine to render an unreliable and inaccurate result, such as...

✓   high body temperature;

✓   GERD/Acid Reflux;

✓   hematocrit issues;

✓   abnormal lung physiology;

✓   improper breathing patterns;

✓   or a partition ratio that is not 2100:1.

The machine is programmed to assume that for every one part of alcohol in a subject's breath, there are 2100 parts in the blood. So the machine does a mathematical calculation to convert breath alcohol concentration to blood-alcohol concentration. However, human beings do not have a constant partition ratio of 2100:1 and partition ratios vary within the human body from 900:1 to about 3400:1.

Urine (Po Po Pee Pee) Test Flaws

There are flaws related to urine testing; AKA, Po Po Pee Pee testing, that lead to inaccurate, and unreliable results. For example, when testing for alcohol:

- ✓ the subject should be required to void (empty) his bladder and wait before giving a reliable urine sample. In my experience, this never takes place. Assuming the Po Po requires the suspect to empty his bladder, an improper time lapse before taking the second urine sample is problematic.

Other problematic factors are:

- ✓ Lack of refrigeration and insufficient use of preservatives for the urine are major problems causing Candida albicans (a pathogenic yeast microbe) contamination;

- ✓ chain of custody issues (problem of how evidence was handled);

- ✓ and equipment calibration, or lack thereof.

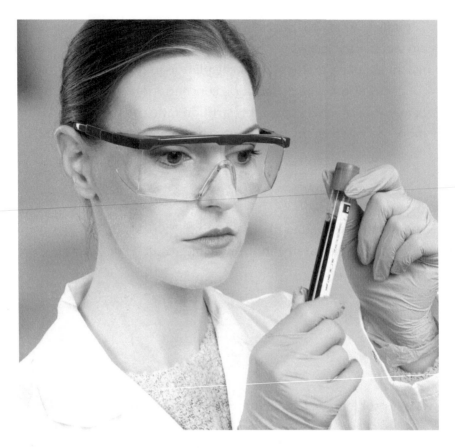

Blood Test Flaws

The same flaws apply in blood testing.

- ✓ Blood samples can be contaminated from bacteria.

- ✓ The phlebotomist taking blood may wipe the skin with an alcohol swab rather than with iodine.

- ✓ Lack of preservatives and lack of refrigeration can cause Candida albicans that contaminate the sample.

- ✓ The sample can be subject to inaccurate analysis and interpretation of the gas chromatogram.

Any of the above factors can lead to an inaccurate result causing your test to produce an inaccurate and falsely high blood alcohol content measurement. As such, you, the suspect player, must **CHOOSE TO REFUSE** and guarantee that the Po Po DUI dealer does not get the chemical test Ace card.

EXPERT WITNESS?

Typically, in challenging the Government's chemical test, you would need an expert witness to properly attack the accuracy, reliability and validity of the result. This is very expensive. Furthermore, **EVEN IF IT'S NOT OVER THE ILLEGAL LIMIT, THE GOVERNMENT STILL CAN PROSECUTE YOU.**

Chemical Test Refusal

With respect to refusing, I want to be clear in informing you that there are **CONSEQUENCES FOR REFUSING A CHEMICAL TEST.** With respect to DUI Blackjack, a refusal of a chemical test is evidence that can be used against you at trial. However, a refusal on its own is unlikely to "bust" your hand and result in a conviction. Furthermore, compared to the evidentiary consequence of a chemical test over the limit, a refusal can be explained away as following the advice of an attorney, and doubting the reliability of the testing, which as discussed above is perfectly reasonable.

However, you must be aware that a refusal carries its own consequences. In both Ohio and Kentucky, the motorists must submit to a chemical test chosen by the law enforcement officer or suffer administrative sanctions.

IN OHIO, those administrative sanctions include an Administrative License Suspension (ALS), with or without privileges, and payment of license reinstatement fees. Note that the ALS also applies for a test at or over the illegal limit. Therefore, the only possibility to avoid this sanction is to submit to the test and test under the illegal limit. Yet even such a test is likely to be offered as evidence against you unless the test shows no alcohol or drugs. **SEE THE CHARTS IN APPENDIX A AND B FOR SPECIFIC CONSEQUENCES OF SUBMITTING OR REFUSING A TEST.**

Particularly for a first-time offender, or even a second time offender, it is worth refusing to preserve not getting an OVI, particularly for an offender who blows at or above the illegal limit of .08. In Ohio, there's also, per se statutory drug levels as well. They are exceptionally low.

IN KENTUCKY, the administrative sanctions include a pre-trial suspension for a first-time offender, whereby the offender may or may not obtain privileges with an ignition interlock device. A driver with a prior conviction within ten years will receive a pre-trial suspension whether they test or not. However, the pre-trial suspension will be credited against the suspension imposed upon any conviction.

WITH RESPECT TO A REPEAT OFFENDER, OHIO LAW ADDS AN ADDITIONAL CONSIDERATION. Within the Ohio OVI statute, 4511.19, the legislature has carved out a separate offense for multiple offenders within a 20 year period. Under this rule, a suspect arrested for OVI who has a prior DUI/OVI or a substantially similar offense within the last 20 years from the date of arrest will be subject to an additional charge called "Refusing to Submit to a Chemical Test." Essentially, if the state adds a charge of refusing to submit to a chemical test, the mandatory minimal jail time increases and the "hard time" suspension without limited driving privileges is longer. **SEE THE CHARTS IN APPENDIX A AND B FOR SPECIFIC CONSEQUENCES OF SUBMITTING OR REFUSING A TEST.**

However, **EVEN WITH RESPECT TO THE REFUSAL CHARGE**, the government must prove both elements of "operation" and "under the influence of alcohol and/or drugs of abuse." If the government cannot prove both of these elements, the suspect will be found **NOT GUILTY** of both offenses. **ONE CAVEAT** of the additional refusal charge is that the state can inform the jury of the prior DUI/OVI offense. Nevertheless, in my experience the consequence of this evidence is much less damaging than a chemical test over the legal limit.

Despite the escalated mandatory minimum sentencing penalties in Ohio for the charge of refusing to submit to a chemical test, I still believe it is in the suspect's best interest to choose to refuse. The suspect who refuses still has a **BETTER CHANCE TO PREVAIL AT TRIAL** because the state will not have chemical test evidence. Evidence is the name of the game in DUI Blackjack. The less evidence that the state has against the suspect, the better chance that the suspect prevails at trial.

Furthermore, **A SUSPECT WHO TESTS AT 0.17 BAC OR HIGHER, WILL ALSO RECEIVE** the escalated mandatory minimum penalty. Because of chemical testing flaws, as indicated in this book, I would not advise taking a chemical test.

Because of this, I still believe it is in the suspect's best interest to choose to refuse even though there may be license sanctions. **BETTER TO ENDURE A LICENSE SANCTION RATHER THAN A CONVICTION OF DUI/OVI, ESPECIALLY FOR A MULTIPLE OFFENDER AND WITH THE SAME THEORY THAT IF THERE IS NO EVIDENCE, IT IS HARDER TO OBTAIN A CONVICTION.** Furthermore, although beyond the scope of this book, the pre-trial license suspension can be appealed and, with the exception of any "hard time" suspension (in Ohio), can frequently be served with privileges for work, school, etc. or ignition interlock.

THE BOTTOM LINE IS THAT, WHILE THERE IS A CONSEQUENCE FOR REFUSING, IT IS FAR LESS THAN THE CONSEQUENCE OF CONVICTION.

Face & Ten Cards: "Standardized" Field Sobriety Tests (SFST's)

3

The roadside tests, called Standardized Field Sobriety Tests (SFSTs), have the potential of a face or ten card. When the Po Po asks the driver to take an SFST, the driver can take the hit, which is equivalent to taking a card. The driver may think to himself, "I'm not impaired I can walk a straight line." In this manner, the driver is thinking he may "draw a low card" because he will do well on the test. However, as in the value of an unseen card, the driver likely does not know all of the factors or clues the Po Po is watching for in conducting the test. While stepping off the line or falling down would be obvious clues, there are more subtle and obscure clues such as not standing in the correct position during the instructions, beginning too soon, and raising arms more than six inches away from the body.

When you agree to "take the hit" of performing SFST's, you are likely to take a 10 or face card (Jack, Queen, King or a 10 card). Nearly every casino blackjack player groans when hit with a face card because it usually leads to a bust. The SFST's are the Horizontal Gaze Nystagmus test, Walk and Turn test, and the One Leg Stand test. Other non-standardized divided attention techniques are the (modified alphabet test, finger count dexterity technique, counting backwards technique), or any other type of "balance technique."

According to the National Highway Traffic Safety Administration **(NHTSA)**, *"there are three SFST's, namely horizontal gaze nystagmus* **(HGN)**, *walk and turn* **(WAT)** *and the one leg stand* **(OLS)**. *Based on a series of controlled laboratory studies, scientifically validated clues of alcohol impairment have been identified for each of these three tests. They are the only standardized field sobriety tests for which validated clues have been identified."*

Horizontal Gaze Nystagmus Test; Walk And Turn Test; One Leg Stand Test;

THE HORIZONTAL GAZE NYSTAGMUS (HGN) is defined by NHSTA as *"involuntary jerking of the eyes occurring as the eyes gaze to the side."*

THE WALK AND TURN is a *"divided attention field sobriety test"* *"where the suspect essentially takes nine heel to toe steps on a real or imaginary line, turns by taking a series of small steps, and takes nine heel to toe steps in the opposite direction".*

THE ONE LEG STAND is also *"divided attention field sobriety test" where the suspect is to raise one leg, either leg, with the foot approximately 6 inches off the ground with the raised foot parallel to the ground as his arms are at his side and counting 1-1000, 2-1000, 3-1000, and so on, until told to stop. The officer must time this test for 30 seconds.*

"DIVIDED ATTENTION TEST"?

A **"DIVIDED ATTENTION TEST"** according to NHTSA"…is a test

which requires the subject to concentrate on both mental and physical tasks at the same time.

"STANDARDIZED"?

The term **"STANDARDIZED"** refers to a method of administering and interpreting SFST's. Standardized tests are supposed to be administered and interpreted in the same manner and under the same conditions, no matter where they take place. The theory is that a cop in Ohio should be able to administer the tests and interpret them in the same manner as in Kentucky. Standardization is not a complex issue. For example, copy paper is standardized at 8 ½ x 11 inches. Many factories have standardized ways of putting their product together to make each product the same way in the same manner. Doing it the same way, every day, without change. Any change would make the product different (see chapter endnote 1 & 2).

A STANDARDIZED TEST IS "one in which the procedures, apparatus, and scoring have been fixed so that precisely the same testing procedures can be followed at different times and places." Cronbach, L., *Essentials Of Psychological Testing*, New York: Harper & Row, 1970.

"VALIDATED"?

The term **"VALIDATED"** refers to the correlation between performance on a SFST and a particular blood-alcohol content. Contrary to what the government says in virtually every state across the nation, the **SFST'S HAVE NO CORRELATION TO IMPAIRMENT.** They merely (and crudely) predict blood alcohol content. Moreover, there is no "pass" or "fail" with regard to SFST's. Isn't that crazy for a "test"? (See chapter endnote 1 & 2)

In addition, **DO NOT CONFUSE** the term **"VALIDATED"** with the term **"VALID."** Validated is the term used by the authors of the National Highway Traffic Safety Administration SFST studies to describe a correlation to a particular blood alcohol content (see chapter endnote 1 & 2).

"VALID"?

"VALID" has the connotation of truth. Prosecutors and police often attempt to portray SFST's as valid indicators of impairment, when they are not (see chapter endnote 1 & 2).

There are **SIX MAJOR STUDIES** regarding field sobriety tests

✓ June, 1977 SFST Study (Southern California Research Institute) *Psychological Tests for DWI Arrests*

✓ March, 1981 SFST Study (Southern California Research Institute) *Development & Field Test of Psychophysical Tests for DWI Arrests*

✓ September, 1983 SFST Study (Office of Driver & Pedestrian Research, Problem-Behavior Research Division) *Field Evaluation of a Behavioral Test Battery for DWI*

✓ Colorado, November 1995 (Southern California Research Institute) *A Colorado Validation Study of the Standardized Field Sobriety Test (SFST) Battery*

✓ San Diego, August 1997 (ANACAPA Sciences, Inc.) *Validation of the Standardized Field Sobriety Test Battery at BACs Below .10 Percent*

✓ Florida, 1998 (Institute of Police Technology & Management, University of North Florida, Pinella's County Sheriff's Office, Southern California Research Institute) *A Florida Validation Study of the Standardized Field Sobriety Test (S.F.S.T.) Battery*

NHTSA Final Validation Study: Revealing Quotes About SFST Reliability!

The final validation study: *Validation Of Standardized Field Sobriety Test Battery At BACs below .10 percent*, August 1997, San Diego; Authors: Jack Stuster And Marcelline Burns; Performing Organization: ANACAPA, Sciences, Inc.; Department Of Transportation Number: DOT HS 808 839. This final validation study contains two critical and important quotes "regarding field sobriety tests"

> *"Horizontal gaze Nystagmus lacks face validity because it does not appear to be linked to the requirements of driving a motor vehicle. The reasoning is correct, but it is based on the incorrect assumption that field sobriety tests are designed to measure driving impairment."*

> *"It is unlikely that complex human performance, such as that required to safely drive an automobile, can be measured at roadside....The link between blood alcohol content and driving impairment is a separate issue, involving entirely different research methods."*

As such, the DUI suspect must **NEVER** volunteer to take these government junk science tests!

HGN-Medical Doctor Test-Not A Po Po Test!

HGN is actually a **MEDICAL TEST** used by doctors to diagnose head injuries and other pathological brain dysfunction. Under the proper circumstances, and with much education, competent medical personnel can use HGN as a diagnostic tool for measuring gross neurological dysfunction. **A TRAFFIC COP HAS NEITHER THE TRAINING NOR THE MEDICAL ACUMEN TO ADMINISTER OR EVALUATE THE HGN EXAM, ESPECIALLY UNDER ENVIRONMENTAL CONDITIONS WHERE A DOCTOR WOULD NEVER ADMINISTER A TEST SUCH AS THIS.** (see chapter endnote 1 & 2)

Furthermore, there are 47 types of Nystagmus. Horizontal gaze nystagmus is merely one of 47. Forty-five of those types of nystagmus have nothing to do with alcohol impairment.

According to NHTSA there are six clues an officer may observe for the HGN test.

- ✓ Lack of Smooth Pursuit in Left Eye

- ✓ Lack of Smooth Pursuit in Right Eye

- ✓ Distinct and sustained nystagmus at maximum deviation in left eye.

- ✓ Distinct and sustained nystagmus at maximum deviation in right eye.

- ✓ Onset of nystagmus prior to 45 degrees in left eye

- ✓ Onset of nystagmus prior to 45 degrees in right eye

According to NHTSA, six out of six cues correlates to a 77% chance that the subject has 0.10 blood alcohol content or higher. In other words, that means in their "studies" there were 23 **FALSE POSITIVES**, or nearly a quarter of the time. **THAT'S NOT GOOD SCIENCE. IN FACT, IT'S GOVERNMENT JUNK SCIENCE.**

Walk & Turn False Positives

On the walk and turn test, there are eight clues that the cop is looking for in attempting to assess the suspect.

- ✓ Cannot keep balance while listening to instructions.
- ✓ Starts before the instructions are finished.
- ✓ Stops while walking.
- ✓ Does not touch heel-to-toe.
- ✓ Steps off the line.
- ✓ Use arms to balance.
- ✓ Improper turn.
- ✓ Incorrect number of steps.

If the suspect has two or more clues on the walk and turn test, or fails to complete it, there is purportedly a 68% chance the suspect is likely to have a blood alcohol content above 0.10. That means 32% are likely not to be above 0.10.

One Leg Stand False Positives

The one leg stand has four clues.

- ✓ The suspect sways while balancing.
- ✓ Uses arms for balance.
- ✓ Hopping.
- ✓ Puts foot down.

According to NHTSA a person who is assessed as having two or more clues has a 65% likelihood of testing above 0.10. On the other hand, 35% will not.

Substantial Compliance Rather Than Strict Compliance? Come On Ohio!

Note that the percentages mention that the suspect will test above or greater than 0.10. Also note, the studies alleging this data assume that the officer strictly complied with the standardized instructions for administering each test. In my experience, most officers do not strictly comply with NHTSA standardized testing instructions. Unfortunately, Ohio requires only "substantial compliance" with NHTSA testing instructions. **APPARENTLY, THE OHIO STATE LEGISLATURE DOES NOT HAVE MUCH FAITH IN THEIR POLICE OFFICERS.**

SOBRIETY - DRUG
PHYSICAL
(MARK 1 TO 2 ITEMS)

A	HAD NOT BEEN DRINKING
B	HBD - UNDER THE INFLUENCE
C	HBD - NOT UNDER INFLUENCE
D	HBD - IMPAIRMENT UNKNOWN
E	UNDER DRUG INFLUENCE*
F	IMPAIRMENT - PHYSICAL*
G	IMPAIRMENT NOT KNOWN

Non-Standardized Po Po Techniques

The additional techniques mentioned by NHTSA such as the alphabet technique, the countdown technique, and the finger count are non-standardized field sobriety techniques (not tests!). They are not validated to correlate to anything. They were not even included in the original studies as possible SFST's to be studied for use in the field. The finger count technique was rejected for use in the three test battery. This test requires people to have good manual hand and finger dexterity, but many people simply do not have good manual finger and hand dexterity. Furthermore, the instructions that the police give on this test are often times confusing (see chapter endnote 1 & 2).

NHTSA Warning Label: "Validity May Be Compromised."

Finally, even NHTSA recognizes that police officers must comply with the standardized instructions, clues, and criteria that are employed to interpret the suspects performance. NHTSA states *"it is necessary to emphasize this validation applies only when:*

- ✓ The tests are administered in the prescribed, standardized manner,

- ✓ The standardized clues are used to assess the suspect's performance,

- ✓ The standardized criteria are employed to interpret that performance,

- ✓ If anyone of the SFST elements is changed, the validity may be compromised."

See revised: DWI Detection and Standardized Field Sobriety Testing 2/2018 Concepts and Principles Of The SFST's (Session 3 Page 10 of 55).

5 Reasons To Choose To Refuse All Field Tests

You must **CHOOSE TO REFUSE** the so-called "standardized field sobriety test" a.k.a. SFST's. In addition, you must also choose to refuse the non-standardized divided attention techniques known as the modified alphabet technique; counting backward technique; and finger count technique, among others.

1. VOLUNTARY TESTS ONLY. First, you need to choose to refuse these so-called divided attention field tests and techniques because they are completely VOLUNTARY! You don't have to do them. The Po Po DUI dealer will attempt to **PSYCHOLOGICAL-LY COERCE YOU** into doing them; or alternatively **MANAGE YOUR IMPRESSION** that you must do them because they know most people want to be compliant to authority and/or police figures. Regardless of the Po Po DUI dealer's tactics, you must not take this "hit." Any so-called tests or techniques such as these are completely voluntary, yet **THE POLICE DO NOT HAVE TO TELL YOU THEY ARE VOLUNTARY.**

2. SUSPECT IS NOT PERMITTED TO STUDY, PREPARE OR PRACTICE BEFORE "TESTS." Why take a test that you have not studied for? In grade school, junior high, high school, college, and law school, we are able to learn the subject matter before being tested. However, with these "tests" you are not permitted to study, prepare, or practice before the testing. **WHY DO A TEST WHEN YOU DO NOT KNOW THE INFORMATION ABOUT THE TEST?** Furthermore, it is unlikely you would know what to study for. **THE SUSPECT DOES NOT KNOW WHAT THE POLICE OFFICER IS LOOKING FOR AS FAR SCORING THE TEST.** In other words, you do not know what is good or bad for purposes

of doing the test correctly. For the DUI Blackjack analogy, this is similar to a casino player who has attempted to count cards and believes the next card dealt will be low, but is surprised to receive a ten, busting his hand. **THE COPS ARE NOT REQUIRED TO TELL YOU WHAT "CLUES" THEY ARE LOOKING FOR IN SCORING THESE TESTS.** If you don't know what the cops are looking for, then how can they ever claim that is a fair test? Obviously, falling down or stepping off the line are inherently obvious from the instructions. However, other clues on the checklist are less obvious and likely to be observed in suspects who have not had a drop of alcohol. For example, beginning a test too soon, not standing correctly prior to beginning a test, and raising arms more than six inches away from the body, are all subtle wrong answers not obvious from the test instructions.

3. **MOST PO PO DUI DEALERS DO NOT KNOW STANDARD-IZED INSTRUCTIONS.** The Government claims, these tests/techniques are "standardized." However, it is exceedingly rare that any Po Po DUI dealer administers these tests strictly using the standardized NHTSA language. As such, if the cops cannot give you the proper standardized instructions, then you are risking having invalid and unreliable test results being introduced at your trial. Moreover, the legislature in Ohio has intervened and said that officers only need to "substantially comply" with the SFST instructions. **IF THERE IS NO STRICT COMPLIANCE WITH NHTSA STANDARDIZED INSTRUCTIONS, THEN HOW CAN THERE BE ANY VALIDITY TO THE TEST RESULTS? THERE CANNOT BE!** Nevertheless, this is a much more difficult burden at trial than it is at roadside where you may simply choose to refuse to perform the SFST's. Do not take the hit of a roadside test.

4. **HIGHLY SUBJECTIVE AND NEGATIVE SCORING SYSTEM.** The scoring of the clues is also highly subjective and often times you cannot see the test on the Po Po DUI dealer cruiser camera to determine whether or not the cop is scoring you properly and accurately. The scoring system is a negative scoring system. In other words, you do not start the test and gain positive points. The cops only score you on what you do poorly. **THEY DO NOT SCORE YOU ON WHAT YOU DO CORRECTLY.** This is a ridiculous way of testing, and this is not the manner in which we were tested in school. **NHTSA SFST STUDIES WERE NOT SCIENTIFICALLY PEER REVIEWED.** Imagine if the casino dealer could look at the card and decide its value when dealing it to you. Do you think you have a good chance of winning the hand?

5. **NO STUDIES FOR DIFFERENT TYPES/GROUPS OF PEOPLE. (NOT EVERYONE IS THE SAME).** The studies surrounding these tests never took into consideration different sexes, ages, physical conditions, health conditions, injuries, etc. **THERE IS NO BASELINE FOR DIFFERENT TYPES OF PEOPLE** in order to make these tests reliable for anyone except for young athletic males or females who were invited to a police academy to be guinea pigs for Po Po field testing. Further, none of the six NHTSA "validation" studies were scientifically peer reviewed.

As such, even if the SFSTs could be considered reliable under the perfect circumstances, for the reasons above, these tests are not reliable in DUI/OVI investigation and are designed for you to fail.

Government Junk Science!

The bottom line: do not volunteer to do these government junk science tests! Not only are they junk science, but they are also voluntary. Who would volunteer to engage in government junk science?? Not me! It should not be you either! Furthermore, because of the "scientific aura" that police officers use to manage society's impression of these tests, you would be gambling on taking these "tests." **SOBER PEOPLE CAN FAIL THESE "TESTS" AS WELL. SO DO NOT TAKE THEM AND RISK GIVING THE GOVERNMENT THIS TYPE OF GOVERNMENT JUNK SCIENCE EVIDENCE.** By choosing to refuse, you are once again guaranteeing that the Po Po DUI dealer does not beat you by getting you to bust your hand! Just say, **"OFFICER, BEFORE I SAY OR DO ANYTHING, I WANT TO TALK TO ATTORNEY STEVEN R. ADAMS."** ▪ ▬ ▬ ▬ ▬ ▬ ▬ ▬ ▬ ▬ ▬ ▬ ▬ ▬ ▬ ◂

---

[1] Steven R. Adams, James Nesci, *Kentucky DUI Defense: The Law and Practice*, Tucson: Lawyers & Judges Publishing Company, Inc., 2018

[2] D. Timothy Huey, Steven R. Adams, James Nesci, *Ohio OVI Defense: The Law and Practice*, Tucson: Lawyers & Judges Publishing Company, Inc., 2016

HE CAN GET'ER DONE. I have known Steve and his work for many years. Not one issue gets by him and he really fights for his clients with zeal and vigor. He is very knowledgeable about criminal law and DUI. The prosecutor has more than he wants or can stand when Steve is on the case.

The Po Po DUI Dealer's Hand

4

There are factors of the DUI stop that are beyond your control, at least by the time of the stop.

THE CIRCUMSTANCES OF THE STOP, such as time of day, day of the week, proximity to a nightclub are factors that can be considered for probable cause and as evidence of guilt.

THE REASON FOR THE STOP, whether a traffic violation, equipment violation, or accident are beyond the driver's control by the time she is pulled over.

THE OFFICER'S OBSERVATIONS of odor of alcohol, slurred speech, and bloodshot eyes, although subjective, are out of the control of the driver.

Accordingly, these are the Po Po DUI dealers cards. Frankly, due to the bias of prosecutors, merely making the arrest gives the officer a pretty good hand. However, there are things you can do to keep this evidence to a minimum.

Traffic And Equipment Violations: 2 Or 3 Card

The first card in the Po PO DUI dealer's hand is the **REASON FOR THE STOP OR INVESTIGATION**. Except in the case of an accident, this is what the police deem to be **"VEHICLE IN MOTION"** evidence. Generally, these are pretty low cards. For example, traffic violations, such as: speed problems, marked lanes violations, stop sign violations, or driving without headlights at night.

These are low numerical cards because I have never been driving where I did not see a person speeding; or crossing a lane line without signaling; or failing to use a turn signal when turning. These driving infractions, and even traffic accidents, occur every single day at every time of the day. These types of infractions do not mean that you are under the influence of alcohol and/or drugs of abuse. However, you can control whether the officer improves his hand. Once the officer asks you about whether you think you committed a traffic violation, don't answer. Again, just say, "OFFICER, BEFORE I SAY OR DO ANYTHING, I WANT TO TALK TO ATTORNEY STEVEN R. ADAMS." It's the cop's burden of proof. Not yours! Just because you may have committed a moving violation or a equipment violation does not mean that you are under the influence of alcohol. Also, you may not have actually committed the technical traffic violation.

Upon my very first phone consultation, Mr. Adams explained things in a way I could understand, and **I WAS PUT AT EASE IMMEDIATELY BY HIS LEGAL KNOWLEDGE, HIS PROFESSIONALISM, AND THE LEVEL OF EXPERIENCE** he demonstrated...Thanks to Mr. Adams, what could have potentially ended my professional career ended up having a positive outcome. He was thorough, kept me well-informed regarding the proceedings of my case, and made me feel like my case was an important to him as it was to myself.

I associate that evidence with a 2 or 3 card. After all, a moving violation is two points in Ohio. That might as well be a 2 card.

"Personal Contact" Evidence

As soon as the officer activates his overhead lights he begins collecting observational or personal contact evidence. This includes how long it takes you to respond to his lights and pull over, where you pull over, and how well you park. After approaching your vehicle, the officer will note odors of alcohol, slurred speech, difficulty retrieving license and insurance, etc. These may amount to numerical cards of 4, 5, 6, 7, 8, or 9. For example, a

- ✓ **4 CARD** may be an odor of alcohol, or marijuana, and the Po Po may see bloodshot eyes.

- ✓ **5 CARD** may be an admission to drinking or smoking marijuana.

- ✓ **8 CARD** may be alleged significant staggering.

- ✓ **9 CARD** may be something said or done that is completely out of the ordinary.

Evidence such as this is called **"OBSERVATIONAL"** or **"PERSONAL CONTACT"** evidence that the police officer seeks to observe or elicit before he decides to have you do field tests. The truth is, this "observational" evidence may be caused by other things besides the effects of alcohol or drugs.

Subjective "Odor," "Bloodshot Eyes" & "Slurred Speech": 4 Card

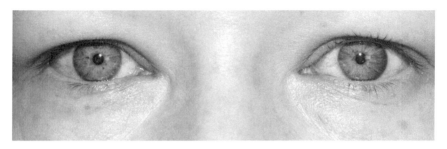

Typically, the police officer approaches a window and has contact with the suspect. In nearly all cases, the cops say that they smell an **"ODOR OF ALCOHOL,"** see **"BLOODSHOT OR WATERY EYES,"** and hear that your **SPEECH IS "SLURRED."** Although speculative and **SUBJECTIVE**, this self-serving observational evidence is used to justify the cop's authority to legally detain the suspect and order him out of the car. Again, I associate this type of evidence to a **4 CARD**. The Po Po DUI dealer may very well get that four card, but so what? I'll bet on that highly subjective, self-serving, alleged evidence any day. **THE KEY IS NOT TO LET THE PO PO GET A BETTER CARD AND NOT TO TAKE A HIT.**

The cop will ask you questions about **WHERE YOU HAVE BEEN, WHERE YOU ARE GOING, AND WHETHER YOU HAVE BEEN DRINKING, ETC. DO NOT ANSWER THESE QUESTIONS. DO NOT LIE ABOUT THESE QUESTIONS EITHER.** Both of these responses can lead to your taking a hit increasing your chance of a bust. If you admit to drinking, that evidence can be used against you. If you are found to be lying, that evidence can be used against you. So don't answer those questions

WHAT DO YOU SAY? Say the following: "OFFICER, BEFORE I SAY OR DO ANYTHING, I WANT TO TALK TO ATTORNEY

" I WAS ISSUED AN OVI CITATION AT A CHECKPOINT

for an empty beer can in the car and a 1 year administrative driving suspension for refusing the breathalyzer test. Steve Adams was able to convince the court to set aside the suspension pending trial that allowed me to continue employment which requires an unrestricted drivers license. He was ultimately successful in getting the entire case dismissed for lack of evidence.

— *Hamilton County Municipal Court, Case No. C/18/TRC/43497* "

STEVEN R. ADAMS." It is highly unlikely that the cop will permit you to call and talk to Steven Adams while his investigation is ongoing. Nevertheless, keep repeating that answer if the officer is insistent. You insist on stating the same answer: **"OFFICER, BEFORE I SAY OR DO ANYTHING, I WANT TO TALK TO ATTORNEY STEVEN R. ADAMS."**

Admissions: 5-6 Card

Also, any **ADMISSIONS TO DRINKING**, **OR COMING FROM A BAR, OR A PARTY,** is evidence the state will use against you. As such, **DO NOT GIVE THEM THAT EVIDENCE**. Remember, the government needs evidence in order to convict you. So do not give them evidence. The Po Po DUI dealer will have less evidence to present to the prosecution to convict you. Evidence of admitting to drinking or using drugs, or using prescriptive medication, could be a 5 OR A 6 CARD, and could give the officer more evidence to better his hand, depending upon the unique circumstances of the case or the information the suspect stated to the police officer. The bottom line is for the suspect not to give the police those cards. You can choose to refuse to give them these extra cards to help them build their hand.

Extra-Ordinary And Unusual Actions: 7, 8 Or 9 Card

This **"OBSERVATIONAL"** evidence would be something extra-ordinary or unusual like...

- ✓ staggering out of the car and falling down
- ✓ or demonstrating complete incoherence or vomiting while admitting to the Po Po you had too much to drink and apologizing.

In summary, by choosing to refuse chemical tests, field tests and techniques, and limiting the officers observational evidence by not making admissions, you avoid taking the hits that will bust your hand, and giving the Po Po additional cards to build their hand. **IMAGINE THAT, YOU THE CITIZEN HAVE THE POWER TO CHOOSE TO REFUSE AND NOT GIVE THE PO PO DUI DEALER EVIDENCE TO BEAT YOU AT DUI BLACKJACK.** By ensuring you don't bust your hand and allowing the Po Po DUI dealer only the cards from a minimal traffic stop and observational evidence, YOU CAN HAVE A VERY WINNABLE HAND OF DUI BLACKJACK.

Steve was unbelievable from the night we called him through the conclusion of the unfortunate event. He explained everything in complete detail, answered all questions straightforwardly and anticipated all expected outcomes. **HE USED HIS YEARS OF EXPERIENCE TO SEEK OUT MISTAKES AND WEAKNESSES IN THE CASE** while leveraging relationships to ensure a just and favorable outcome for me. I could not be happier with his representation and my ultimate outcome.

3 Wild Cards for the DUI Blackjack Suspect/Player

5

There are no wild cards in casino Blackjack. Nevertheless, for purposes of you gaining an additional advantage in playing and participating in DUI Blackjack, I am going to assume that there are three wild cards that you want to have in your possession when playing against the Po Po DUI dealer. So get the following DUI Blackjack "wild cards"!

- ✓ **Provide the Po Po with license, insurance and registration if asked.**

- ✓ **Exit your car when asked.**

- ✓ **Do not resist arrest.**

1. **PROVIDE THE PO PO WITH LICENSE, INSURANCE AND REGISTRATION IF ASKED.** Furtive movements inside the car may cause the officer concern that the driver is getting a weapon. This may be especially true if the driver has a concealed carry permit. If so, you must tell the officer about that immediately. The best advice is to keep your insurance card and registration in the console, on top of other contents of the glove box, or another readily-accessible area so you do not have to fumble through documents for them. In that case, if the license and registration can be obtained quickly and without much movement inside the car, the driver could put down his window, turn on the light, obtain the documentation, and have his hands on the steering wheel by the time the officer arrives at the vehicle. **BY LAW, YOU MUST IDENTIFY YOURSELF.** These documents will do that. By law, you must be driving with insurance and your car must be registered in a state. **AS SUCH, HAVE THESE DOCUMENTS READILY ACCESSIBLE BEFORE THE PO PO DUI DEALER APPROACHES.** Once he approaches, he will ask you for this information and you will be able to give it to him immediately. Some of the clues that the Po Po DUI Dealer is looking for in this part of his investigation are whether or not you fumble these documents, provide the wrong documents, drop the documents, or do not follow directions in order to obtain them. Make sure you have these available!

2. **EXIT YOUR CAR WHEN ASKED.** Exiting your vehicle when told to do so. By law, the Po Po DUI Dealer can and most likely will, ask you to exit your vehicle. **YOU MUST EXIT.** In Ohio, if you do not exit the car, you can be charged with obstructing official business for impeding a police investigation. Furthermore, the Po Po DUI Dealer can get you out of the car in order to ensure that you have no weapons for their safety. As such, politely get out of the car when you are instructed to do so.

    Obstructing a Official Business is a misdemeanor of the second degree in Ohio and carries up to 90 days in jail and up to a $750 fine. Beware!

3. **DO NOT RESIST ARREST.** Do Not Resist Arrest. You may not get arrested. However, based upon my 30 years of experience in prosecuting and defending crimes, you will get arrested. But do not resist arrest. Be polite and be nice. Resisting arrest **IN OHIO** is a misdemeanor of the first degree that carries 0 to 180 days and up to $1000 fine. **IN KENTUCKY**, resisting arrest is a class A misdemeanor carrying a penalty of up to 12 months in jail and up to a $500 fine. Be polite and nice and do not resist arrest. Let the Po Po DUI Dealer be abrasive and impolite—Not You! Take possession of that wild card.

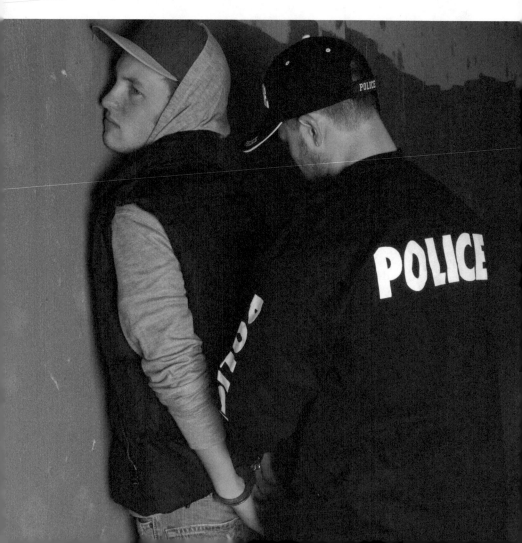

Government's Burden: Proof Beyond A Reasonable Doubt

6

In the United States of America, the government (the police and prosecution) have a very high and difficult burden of proof. **THE BURDEN OF PROOF BEYOND A REASONABLE DOUBT.**

Ohio Definition

In Ohio, proof beyond a reasonable doubt is defined as follows:

> *Reasonable doubt is present when, after you have carefully considered and compared all the evidence, you cannot say you are firmly convinced of the truth of the charge. Reasonable doubt is a doubt based on reason and common sense. Reasonable doubt is not mere possible doubt, because everything relating to human affairs or depending on moral evidence is open to some possible or imaginary doubt. Proof beyond a reasonable doubt is proof of such character that an ordinary person would be willing to rely and act upon it in the most important of his/her own affairs.*

Kentucky Definition

In, Kentucky, **PROOF BEYOND A REASONABLE DOUBT IS NOT DEFINED**. It is up to the jury to define it.

There are other legal burdens such as a reasonable suspicion, probable cause, a preponderance of the evidence, clear and convincing evidence, and reasonable doubt. However, the state must surpass these burdens. They must prove that the accused drove under the influence of alcohol and/or drug of abuse by proof **BEYOND** a reasonable doubt. As such, even if there is one reason to doubt the guilt of the accused, the jury must acquit and find that person not guilty.

I BELIEVE IT WAS STEVE'S COMPREHENSIVE PREPARATION and detailed knowledge of the law that allowed the jury to clearly see through to the facts of my case.

DUI/OVI: A Crime Of "Opinion"

7

In Ohio, Kentucky, and any other states in America, DUI is the only crime where a citizen can be convicted by one police officer's opinion. An **OPINION** is a view or judgment formed about something, not necessarily based on fact or knowledge.

As we all know, different people may draw opposing conclusions, even if they agree on the same set of facts. Also, an opinion may be the result of a person's feelings, beliefs, and desires mixed in with their personal bias or agenda. Some opinions, such as scientific opinions may reflect opinions on scientific or technical issues, published in scholarly journals, which entail peer-reviewed and rigorous professional editing. Even scientific opinions can be partial, conflicting, and uncertain. Opinions must be based on facts (the more facts the better). If the DUI Blackjack player does not give the Po Po DUI dealer facts in order to substantiate his opinion that he is under the influence, then the DUI Blackjack player has an advantage in prevailing; i.e. **NOT GUILTY!**

If the Po Po DUI dealer does not get Blackjack against the player/suspect then that man or woman must be a acquitted and found not guilty. There is simply no proof beyond a reasonable doubt. This is certainly true if the DUI Blackjack player does not provide evidence, and exercises their right in the United States of America to be presumed innocent, remain silent, and have the government prove their guilt by proof beyond a reasonable doubt (rather than helping the government). **THERE IS NO LAW THAT SAYS A CITIZEN SUSPECTED OF A CRIME HAS TO HELP THE GOVERNMENT IN THEIR INVESTIGATION OF THE FACTS. SO DON'T!** And if you choose to refuse and say No No to the Po Po DUI dealer, you certainly increase the probabilities of securing an acquittal and hearing the jury say Not Guilty!

Without evidence on a crime of opinion, that is, the police officer's opinion, it is a very difficult burden of proof for the government. If the officer does not have solid, significant, and credible evidence to support his opinion, then the burden of proof becomes much more difficult for the government. In Ohio, Kentucky and in America, **THE ACCUSED DOES NOT HAVE TO HELP THE GOVERNMENT GET EVIDENCE; DOES NOT HAVE TO TESTIFY; DOES NOT HAVE TO VOLUNTEER EVIDENCE; DOES NOT HAVE TO PRESENT EVIDENCE BY WAY OF DOCUMENTS, TESTIMONY, OR EXPERT WITNESSES. THE GOVERNMENT HAS THE EXCLUSIVE BURDEN OF PROOF.** The jury is instructed that there is no obligation for the accused to put on any evidence, and the jury cannot hold that against the accused. The jury must focus on what, if any, evidence, the state has to support the allegation of driving under the influence of alcohol. And they must do so applying the standard of proof beyond a reasonable doubt.

Under the Influence in Ohio

The Ohio Jury instructions for *Under the influence* is:

Under the influence means that the defendant consumed some (alcohol)(drug of abuse)(alcohol and a drug of abuse), whether mild or potent, in such a quantity, whether small or great, that it adversely affected and appreciably impaired the defendant's actions, reactions, or mental processes under the circumstances then existing and deprived him of that clearness of intellect and control of himself which he would otherwise have possessed.

The question is not how much (alcohol)(drug of abuse) (alcohol and a drug of abuse) would affect an ordinary person. The question is what effect did any (alcohol)(drug of abuse) (alcohol and a drug of abuse), consumed by the defendant, have on him at the time and place involved.

If the consumption of (alcohol)(drug of abuse)(alcohol and a drug of abuse) so affected the nervous system, brain, or muscles of the defendant so as to impair, to an appreciable degree, his ability to operate the vehicle, then the defendant was under the influence.

Under the influence in Kentucky

In Kentucky, under the influence of alcohol or drugs of abuse is not statutorily defined. It is up to the jury to define what "under the influence" means.

Therefore, if the suspect lawfully chooses to refuse to give evidence, and appears to be alert, coherent, and able to communicate well with the Po Po DUI dealer in an understandable way, then she can appear to be **UN-INFLUENCED BY ALCOHOL OR A DRUG OF ABUSE!**

Recall the previous Ohio definition, reasonable doubt "is present when, after you have carefully considered and compared all the evidence, you cannot say you are firmly convinced of the truth of the charge."

REASONABLE DOUBT is a doubt based on reason and common sense.

Reasonable doubt is not mere possible doubt, because everything relating to human affairs, or depending on moral evidence is open to some possible or imaginary doubt.

PROOF BEYOND A REASONABLE DOUBT IS PROOF OF SUCH CHARACTER THAT AN ORDINARY PERSON WOULD BE WILLING TO RELY AND ACT UPON IT IN THE MOST IMPORTANT OF HIS/HER OWN AFFAIRS. In other words, would you believe that the accused is guilty of operating a motor vehicle while under the influence of alcohol that the Po Po DUI dealer merely had a two card and a four card? Or, even a 2 card and a 9 card?

The reason for proof beyond a reasonable doubt is clear in America. John Adams said it himself in 1770 just prior to our country gaining independence. After successfully representing the "redcoats" at the Boston Massacre Trial, he said, "A COMMUNITY GAINS MORE BY PROTECTING INNOCENCE THAN BY PUNISHING GUILT." That is the reason for the presumption of innocence in Ohio, Kentucky, and America when the accused is charged with a crime. It is critical that our system of justice prevents wrongful convictions.

Our Founding Fathers Had Much to Say About Opinions

In 1801, Thomas Jefferson, in a letter to Sam Adams, wrote,

"opinion and the just maintenance of it, shall never be a crime in my view; nor bring injury on the individual."

In 1798 President George Washington, in a letter to George Custis, wrote,

"conjectures are often substituted for fact."

In 1787, James Madison made a speech to the Constitutional Convention and said,

"all men having power ought to be distrusted to a certain degree."

John Adams in a letter to Thomas Jefferson said,

"power must never be trusted without a check."

Finally, John Adams also said after the Boston Massacre Trial that

"facts are stubborn things; and whatever may be our wishes, our inclinations, or the dictates of our passions, they cannot alter the state of facts and evidence"

"When we went to trial, **HE EXCEEDED ALL OF MY EXPECTATIONS** in the way he must have meticulously prepared. I saw his dedication first hand."

"If you want a guy that **FIGHTS HARD AND GOES THE EXTRA MILE** to get 'not guilty,' this is your man!"

DUI Blackjack in Action

- ✓ State v. J.D.

- ✓ State v. L.S.

- ✓ State v. R.S.

DISCLAIMER: Prior results do not guarantee a similar outcome in your case.

STATE v. J.D.

JD rear-ended another car on the highway. The investigating cop arrived, and according to his report he smelled alcohol, observed bloodshot watery eyes and other signs of intoxication. When the Po Po DUI Dealer asked JD if he had been drinking, JD "took a hit" when he admitted to drinking. However, when asked to perform field tests and a chemical test, JD wisely declined to "take a hit". JD was arrested for DUI/OVI. After being arrested but before being released, JD appeared to have wet his pants. At trial, the investigating officer testified to the following as it relates to JD:

- ✓ **JD was coherent but confused.**

- ✓ **JD took a while to retrieve his license.**

- ✓ **JD's person smelled of alcohol.**

- ✓ **JD admitted to consuming 3 to 4 beers.**

- ✓ **JD had watery and bloodshot eyes.**

- ✓ **JD was unsteady on his feet.**

- ✓ **While standing in place, JD was swaying.**

- ✓ **JD exhibited slurred speech.**

- ✓ **JD refused to engage in field testing.**

- ✓ **The cop had noticed that JD had "wet" his pants after the arrest.**

- ✓ **JD refused to take a breath test.**

STATE v. J.D.

The State came to court with a hand built on a traffic accident, observational evidence, and an admission to drinking. However, JD avoided going bust by refusing all field tests and chemical tests. Steve Adams cross-examined the arresting officer and elicited the following: it is common to be confused when an accident occurred on the Highway; JD's license was stuck in the plastic window casing of his wallet; the cop acknowledged that the odor of alcoholic coming from a person does not that mean the person is under the influence of alcohol; the cop did not know the timeline that JD drank 3 to 4 beers; the cop acknowledged that the timeline is important and that he should have asked about that timeline; the cop acknowledged it is not uncommon to have watery bloodshot eyes at night; the cop could not articulate specifically how JD was unsteady on his feet or swaying in place; the cop acknowledged that JD did not fall down or almost fall down. Furthermore, the cop acknowledged that field testing is voluntary.

In addition, the cop acknowledged that JD was requesting to use the restroom for an extended period of time and that he asked the cop to use the restroom more than once after his arrest. The cop also acknowledged that JD had a right to refuse a breath test.

After closing argument, JD was found NOT GUILTY of OVI/DUI.

– Hamilton County Municipal Court, Case No.: C/19/TRC/8224

STATE v. L.S.

In this case LS rear-ended another car. The police were called and completed their investigation where, as usual, they allegedly smelled an odor of alcohol and observed bloodshot eyes. LS denied drinking and refused to complete the HGN test and refused additional field tests. She was arrested for DUI/OVI and refused to take a breath test.

This case subsequently went to trial where the arresting officer testified to the following:

- ✓ He smelled an odor of alcohol on LS's person.

- ✓ LS had bloodshot eyes.

- ✓ LS denied drinking alcoholic beverages.

- ✓ LS refused to complete the horizontal gaze nystagmus test (eye test.)

- ✓ LS refused to take a breath test.

STATE v. L.S.

The State came to court with a hand built on a minor traffic accident, observational evidence, and a breath test refusal. However, LS avoided busting her hand by refusing to complete the HGN test and refusing to submit to a chemical test. On cross-examination, Steve Adams sought to minimize the cop's subjective observations and elicited from the cop that it is not uncommon for people to have bloodshot eyes. He further elicited that the field tests are completely voluntary, and that LS had a right to refuse to complete the horizontal gaze nystagmus test.

In addition, the cop testified that LS spoke and communicated well; walked around the scene without any problems; and was fully insured. Moreover, the cop testified that there was no insurance claim because there was no damage to the other car as a result of this rear end bump.

After closing argument, LS was subsequently found NOT GUILTY of OVI/DUI.

– *Clermont County Municipal Court, Case No.: 2018TRC12593*

STATE v. R.S.

Cop was parked in a parking spot on a one-way street. Late at night, cop noticed RS travel by him at a high rate of speed. As he was watched RS drive by, he subsequently testified that RS was squealing his tires and did not come to a complete stop when making a left-hand turn on red. He radioed for a backup officer who was within a half block from RS. RS parked his car nearby. The backup officer approached RS based upon the description given by the initial officer's report. The initial officer came to the scene and identified RS's car as the car that was driving "recklessly". The backup-cop then testified that RS demonstrated the following:

- ✓ RS had watery eyes.
- ✓ RS could not follow instructions like "look at me" and "keep your hands out of your pocket"
- ✓ RS could not say his alphabet completely.
- ✓ RS smelled of alcohol.

Upon cross-examination, the initial reporting officer testified that he did not know the speed limit of the one-way street. Furthermore, he could not estimate RS's "high rate of speed."

The officer also acknowledged that in the video, from a distance, it appeared that RS was using his brakes because you could see brake lights and RS coming to a stop at a red light. The cop acknowledged that RS used his turn signal and, later, properly parked his car.

The cop also acknowledged that there were no pedestrians crossing the street during this time and RS did not almost cause an accident or crash into property.

STATE v. R.S.

The backup officer testified that RS had no problems exiting his car. The copy further testified that RS was steady when walking and standing; that he had control of himself; and that he didn't have any balance problems or unsteadiness about him.

Further, the backup-cop testified that:

- ✓ RS did not have bloodshot eyes;

- ✓ That neither cop asked RS whether or not he had been drinking alcoholic beverages;

- ✓ That the smell of alcohol was coming from RS's breath;

- ✓ When he instructed RS to take his hands out of his pockets he did so.

- ✓ He never told him to "always keep them out of his pocket".

- ✓ Finally, RS told the officers that he was not intoxicated.

- ✓ Other than the informal alphabet technique, RS did not engage in other field testing.

- ✓ RS also refused a breath test.

After closing argument, RS was found NOT GUILTY of OVI/DUI and also NOT GUILTY of reckless operation. RS refused the SFST's and refused the breath test. RS's successful outcome in DUI Blackjack was the result of refusing to be coerced into taking hits to bust his hand.

– *Hamilton County Municipal Court, Case No.: 18/TRC/21818*

Conclusion

DUI Blackjack is about refusing to give the State the evidence it needs to convict a driver of DUI. While I do not endorse or approve of driving while impaired, I am also aware that many unimpaired drivers are arrested for and convicted of DUI/OVI. This is because DUI is a crime of opinion and the methods used to gather evidence are biased in favor of convictions. In casino Blackjack, a player with a strategy increases his chances of beating the house. Applying the theory of DUI Blackjack will allow a suspect to minimize his chance of going bust and increase the chance of being found NOT GUILTY. Using the above principles and guidelines will avoid giving the State evidence and minimize the chance that they can wrongfully convict you, a loved one, or a friend of OVI/DUI.

Appendix A: Ohio OVI/ DUI Penalty Charts

Ohio Penalty Charts

PRIOR OVI OFFENSES?	OFFENSE TYPE	JAIL TIME, IF ANY	FINES	ALCOHOL/DRUG TREATMENT	
1ST IN 10 YEARS (OVI, low test or drug)	M-1	3 days in jail or DIP. Up to 6 months1	$375-$1,075	Optional	
1ST IN 10 YEARS AND EITHER: [a] high test OR [b] refusal with prior in 20 years	M-1	6 days in jail or 3 days in jail and DIP. Up to 6 months1	$375-$1,075	Optional	
2ND IN 10 YEARS (OVI, low test or drug)	M-1	10 days in jail or 5 days in jail and 18 days HAEM² and/ or CAM.³ Up to 6 months	$525-$1,625	Alcohol/ drug assessment recommended, treatment mandatory	
2ND IN 10 YEARS AND EITHER: [a] high test OR [b] refusal with prior in 20 years	M-1	20 days jail or 10 days jail and 36 days HAEM² and/ or CAM³. Up to 6 months.	$525-$1,625	Alcohol/ drug assessment recommended, Treatment mandatory	
3RD IN 10 YEARS (OVI, low test or drug)	Unclassified Misdemeanor	30 days in jail or 15 days in jail and 55 days HAEM² and/or CAM³. Up to 1 year	$850-$2,750	Alcohol/ drug addiction program mandatory	
3RD IN 10 YEARS AND EITHER: [a] high test OR [b] refusal with prior in 20 years	Unclassified Misdemeanor	60 days in jail or 30 days in jail and 110 days HAEM² and/or CAM³. Up to 1 year	$850-$2,750	Alcohol/ drug addiction program mandatory	
EITHER: [a] 4th or 5th in 10 years OR [b] 6th in 20 years (OVI, low test or drug)	F-4	60 days local incarceration, up to 1 year; or 60 days prison with option of additional 6-30 months	$1,350-$10,500	Alcohol/ drug addiction program mandatory	
EITHER: [a] 4th or 5th in 10 years OR [b] 6th in 20 years (and high test or refusal)	F-4	120 days local incarceration, up to 1 year; or 120 days prison, with option of additional 6-30 months	$1,350-$10,500	Alcohol/ drug addiction program mandatory	
2ND FELONY LIFETIME (and, low test or drug)	F-3	60 days prison, up to 36 months	$1,350-$10,500	Alcohol/ drug addiction program mandatory	
2ND FELONY LIFETIME AND EITHER: [a] high test OR [b] refusal	F-3	120 days prison. Up to 36 months	$1,350-$10,500	Alcohol/ drug addiction program mandatory	
1ST OR 2ND FELONY LIFETIME WITH RC 2941.1413 specification⁴	F-4 (1st felony) F-3 (2nd felony)	1-5 years prison to be served prior and consecutive to any F-4 or F-3 penalties set forth in boxes above and which may be imposed	$1,350-$10,500	Alcohol/ drug addiction program mandatory	

DL: Interlock Driver's License
IID: Ignition Interlock Device
DIP: Drivers Intervention Program
¹ Must suspend jail if defendant is granted unlimited driving privileges
² **HAEM:** House Arrest and Electronic Monitoring (required finding that jail is overcrowded)
³ **CAM:** Continuous Alcohol Monitoring (required finding that jail is overcrowded)

OVI ORC 4511.19 (6 POINTS ON LICENSE)

LICENSE SUSPENSION	DISCRETIONARY DRIVING PRIVILEGES	IID AND/OR RESTRICTED PLATES	IMMOBILIZATION/ FORFEITURE OF VEHICLE	REINSTATEMENT FEE
1 to 3 years	After 15 days	Plates optional, DL/ IID required*	No	$475.00
1 to 3 years	After 15 days (30 day ALS[5] if Refusal)	Plates required, DL/ IID required*	No	$475.00
1 to 7 years	After 45 days	Plates optional, DL/ IID required**	Immobilize 90 days if registered to defendant	$475.00
1 to 7 years	After 45 days (90 day ALS[5] if refusal)	Plates required for high test, optional for refusal. DL/ IIC required**	Immobilize 90 days if registered to defendant	$475.00
2 to 12 years (minimum may be reduced to 1 year)	After 180 days	Plates required, DL/ IID required**	Forfeit if registered to defendant	$475.00
2 to 12 years (minimum may be reduced to 1 year)	After 180 days	Plates required, DL/ IID required**	Forfeit if registered to defendant	$475.00
3 years to life	After 3 years	Plates required, DL/ IID required**	Forfeit if registered to defendant	$475.00
3 years to life	After 3 years	Plates required, DL/ IID required**	Forfeit if registered to defendant	$475.00
3 years to life	After 3 years	Plates required, DL/ IID required**	Forfeit if registered to defendant	$475.00
3 years to life	After 3 years	Plates required, DL/ IID required**	Forfeit if registered to defendant	$475.00
3 years to life	After 3 years	Plates required, DL/ IID required**	Forfeit if registered to defendant	$475.00

Specification: "Within 20 years the Offender has previously pleaded guilty or been convicted of 5 or more equivalent Offenses
[5]**ALS:** Administration License Suspension Imposed by Ohio BMV.
*Required with unlimited privileges
**Required if alcohol related, optional if drug related

Ohio Alcohol And Drug Impaired Driving Law Per Se Offense Types

Operation under the influence of alcohol, drug abuse, or both. ORC 4511.19 (A)(1)(a)

Operation with concentration of alcohol as specified below. ORC 4511.19 (A)(1)(b-i)

ALCOHOL LEVEL	WHOLE BLOOD		BLOOD SERUM OR PLASMA		BREATH		URINE	
LOW TEST	≥ .08% < .17%	§(A)(1)(b)	≥ .96% <.204%	§(A)(1)(c)	≥ .08g < .17g	§(A)(1)(d)	≥ .11g < .238g	§(A)(1)(e)
HIGH TEST	≥ .17%	§(A)(1)(f)	≥.204%	§(A)(1)(g)	≥ .17g	§(A)(1)(h)	≥ .238g	§(A)(1)(i)

CONTROLLED SUBSTANCE	URINE	WHOLE BLOOD, BLOOD SERUM, OR PLASMA	SECTION NO.
AMPHETAMINE	≥ 500 ng	≥ 100 ng	§(A)(1)(j)(i)
COCAINE	≥ 150 ng	≥ 50 ng	§(A)(1)(j)(ii)
COCAINE METABOLITE	≥ 150 ng	≥ 50 ng	§(A)(1)(j)(iii)
HEROIN	≥ 2000 ng	≥ 50 ng	§(A)(1)(j)(iv)
HEROIN METABOLITE	≥ 10 ng	≥ 10 ng	§(A)(1)(j)(v)
LSD	≥ 25 ng	≥ 10 ng	§(A)(1)(j)(vi)
MARIJUANA	≥ 10 ng	≥ 2 ng	§(A)(1)(j)(vii)
MARIJUANA METABOLITE AND UNDER THE INFLUENCE	≥ 15 ng	≥ 5 ng	§(A)(1)(j)(viii)(I)
MARIJUANA METABOLITE	≥ 35 ng	≥ 50 ng	§(A)(1)(j)(viii)(II)
METHAMPHETAMINE	≥ 500 ng	≥ 100 ng	§(A)(1)(j)(ix)
PHENCYCLIDINE	≥ 25 ng	≥ 10 ng	§(A)(1)(j)(x)
SALVIA DIVINORUM AND SALVINORIN A	To be specified by State Board of Pharmacy Rule	To be specified by State Board of Pharmacy Rule	§(A)(1)(j)(xi)

Operation with concentration of controlled substance as specified below. ORC 4511.19 (A)(1)(j)(i)-(xi)

Operation under the influence of alcohol, drug of abuse or both with prior OVI conviction in 20 years, and with current refusal of chemical tests. ORC 4511.19 (A)(2)

Operation by person under age 21 with concentration of alcohol as specified below

WHOLE BLOOD		BLOOD SERUM OR PLASMA		BREATH		URINE	
≥ .02% < .08%	§(B)(1)	≥ .03% < .096%	§(B)(2)	≥ .02G < .08G	§(B)(3)	≥ .028G < .11G	§(B)(4)

Having physical control while under the influence of alcohol, drug of abuse or both, or with concentration of alcohol or controlled substance equal to or greater than §(A)(1)(b-e) or (j) amounts. ORC 4511.194 (B)(1-3)

Ohio Administrative License Suspension

REFUSAL OF CHEMICAL TEST ORC 4511.191 (B)

REFUSAL/ CONVICTIONS IN 10 YEARS	LENGTH OF SUSPENSION	DISCRETIONARY DRIVING PRIVILEGES	RESTRICTED PLATES	RESTRICTED LICENSE/ IID
1ST	1 year	After 30 days	Optional	Optional
2ND	2 years	After 90 days	Optional	Optional
3RD	3 years	After 1 year	Optional	Optional
4TH OR MORE	5 years	After 3 years	Optional	Optional

FAILED CHEMICAL TEST ORC 4511.191 (C)

NO. OF OFFENSE IN 10 YEARS	LENGTH OF SUSPENSION	DISCRETIONARY DRIVING PRIVILEGES	RESTRICTED PLATES	RESTRICTED LICENSE/ IID
1ST	90 days	After 15 days	Optional	Optional
2ND	1 year	After 45 days	Optional	Optional
3RD	2 years	After 180 days	Optional	Required if alcohol related, optional if drug
4TH OR MORE	3 years	After 3 years	Optional	Required if alcohol related, optional if drug

IID: Ignition Interlock Device

Ohio Underage Alcohol And Drug Impaired Driving Law Per Se Offense Types

Operation under the influence of alcohol, drug abuse, or both. ORC 4511.19 (A)(1)(a)

Operation with concentration of alcohol as specified below. ORC 4511.19 (A)(1)(b-i)

PRIOR OVI OFFENSES?	OFFENSE TYPE	JAIL TIME, IF ANY?	FINES	ALCOHOL/ DRUG TREATMENT	
1ST IN 1 YEAR	M-4	0-30 days jail	$0-$250	Optional	
2ND OR MORE IN 1 YEAR	M-3	0-60 days jail	$0-$500	Optional	

The Underage per se limit is **0.02** blood alcohol content or above

IID: Ignition Interlock Device

IMMOBILIZATION / FORFEITURE: Not applicable.

	MANDATORY LICENSE SUSPENSION	DISCRETIONARY DRIVING PRIVILEGES	IID / RESTRICTED LICENSE	REINSTATEMENT FEE
	90 days to 2 years	After 60 days	License/ Interlock required with unlimited privileges	$40
	1-5 years	After 60 days	Optional	$40

Ohio
Physical Control While
Under The Influence
RC 4511.194

PRIOR OFFENSES?	OFFENSE TYPE	JAIL TIME, IF ANY?	FINES	ALCOHOL/ DRUG TREATMENT	
Any	M-1	0-180 days jail	$0-$1,000	Optional	

PHYSICAL CONTROL means being in the driver's position of the front seat of a vehicle and having possession of the vehicle's ignition key or other ignition device.

NOTE: Unlike OVI/DUI there is no element of "operation"

IID: Ignition Interlock Device

IMMOBILIZATION / FORFEITURE: Not applicable

	LICENSE SUSPENSION	DISCRETIONARY DRIVING PRIVILEGES	IID / RESTRICTED LICENSE	REINSTATEMENT FEE
	Up to 1 year	No "hard time"	Optional	$475.00

Ohio
RC 4510.14—Driving Under
OVI Suspension—6 points

PRIOR OFFENSES?	OFFENSE TYPE	MANDATORY JAIL TIME	FINES	POTENTIAL RESTITUTION FOR LOSS DUE TO ACCIDENT	
First in 6 years	M-1	3-180 days jail Or 30-180 days HAEM	$250-$1000	Up to $5000 If no proof of Δ's Insurance	
Second In 6 years	M-1	10 days 1 year jail Or 90 days to 1 year HAEM	$500-$2500	Up to $5000 If no proof of Δ's Insurance	
Third or more In 6 years	Misdemeanor	30 days to 1year jail No HAEM	$500-$2500	Up to $5000 If no proof of Δ's Insurance	

Δ = Defendant

HAEM = House Arrest and Electronic Monitoring

	SUSPENSION (UP TO 1 YEAR)	IMMOBILIZATION	FORFEITURE	IMPOUNDMENT OF PLATES REQUIRED
	Mandatory	Mandatory 30 Days if Δ owns vehicle	NO	Mandatory 30 days if Δ owns vehicle
	Mandatory	Mandatory 60 Days if Δ owns vehicle	NO	Mandatory 60 days if Δ owns vehicle
	Mandatory	NO	Mandatory if Δ owns vehicle	Optional if Δ Owns vehicle

Appendix B: Kentucky DUI Penalty Charts

Kentucky DUI Penalties for Being in Physical Control or Operating a Motor Vehicle While Under the Influence (KRS §189A.010)

NUMBER OF OFFENSE	DEGREE OF OFFENSE	INCARCERATION	FINES	TREATMENT	
1ST IN 10 YEARS	Unclassified Misdemeanor	0-30 days	$200-$500	Required (90 days)	
1ST IN 10 YEARS + AGGRAVATOR[3]	Unclassified Misdemeanor	4-30 days	$250-$500	Required	
2ND IN 10 YEARS	Unclassified Misdemeanor	7 days to 6 months	$350-$500	Required (1 year)	
2ND IN 10 YEARS + AGGRAVATOR[3]	Unclassified Misdemeanor	14 days to 6 months	$350-$500	Required	
3RD IN 10 YEARS	Unclassified Misdemeanor	30 days to 1 year	$500-$1,000	Required (1 year)	
3RD IN 10 YEARS + AGGRAVATOR[3]	Unclassified Misdemeanor	60 days to 1 year	$500-$1,000	Required	
4TH OR > IN 10 YEARS	Class D Felony	1-5 years. Min. 120 days	$1,000-$10,000	Required	
4TH OR > IN 5 YEARS + AGGRAVATOR[3]	Class D Felony	1-5 years. Min. 240 days	$1,000-$10,000	Required (1 year)	

1: KRS § 189A. 430 (1) "The cabinet, upon written order of the District Court, shall deliver to the defendant a permit card setting forth the times, places, purposes, and other conditions limiting the defendant's use of a motor vehicle" However, pursuant to KRS §189a.410 (3): the court shall not issue a hardship license to a person who refused to take an alcohol concentration or substance test or tests offered by a law enforcement officer.

2: KRS § 189A.070 (7) After a minimum of twelve (12) months from the effective date of the revocation one may move the court to reduce the period of revocation on a day-for-day basis for each day the person held a valid ignition interlock license under KRS 189A.420, but in no case shall the reduction reduce the period of ignition interlock use to less than twelve (12) months.

LICENSE SUSPENSION	DRIVING PRIVILEGES	IMMOBILIZATION/ FORFEITURE	RESTRICTED PLATES FOR PRIVILEGES
30-120 days	After 30 days	No	Decal and permit card[1]
30-120 days	After 30 days	No	Decal and permit card[1]
12-18 months	None	Mandatory	Reduction of Suspension[2]
12-18 months	None	Mandatory	Reduction of Suspension[2]
24-36 months	None	Mandatory	Reduction of Suspension[2]
24-36 months	None	Mandatory	Reduction of Suspension[2]
60 months	None	Mandatory	Reduction of Suspension[2]
60 months	None	Mandatory	Reduction of Suspension[2]

3: KRS§189A.010 (11)(a)-(f) (a) operating a motor vehicle in excess of thirty (30) miles per hours above the speed limit; (b) Operating a motor vehicle in the wrong direction on a limited access highway; (c) Operating a motor vehicle that causes an accident resulting in death or serious physical injury as defined in KRS 500.080; (d) Operating a motor vehicle while the alcohol concentration in the operator's blood or breath is 0.15 or more as measured by a test or tests of a sample of the operator's blood or breath taken two (2) hours after a cessation of operation of the motor vehicle; (e) Refusing to submit to any test or tests of one's blood, breath, or urine requested by an officer having reasonable grounds to believe the person was operating or in physical control of a motor vehicle of in violation of subsection (1) of this section; an (f) Operating a motor vehicle that is transporting a passenger under the age of twelve (12) years old

Kentucky DUI Penalties for Being in Physical Control or Operating a Motor Vehicle After Underage Consumption of Alcohol (KRS §189A.010)

NUMBER OF OFFENSES	DEGREE OF OFFENSE	INCARCERATION	FINES	TREATMENT	
All	Unclassified Misdemeanor	Fine Only	$100-$500	Required	

*6 months or until age 18, whichever is longer

**30 days to 6 months

1: After 30 days

2: May apply for interlock device after 1 year

3: Under 21 per se limit is 0.02 Blood Alcohol Content or above

	MANDATORY LICENSE SUSPENSION	DRIVING PRIVILEGES	IMMOBILIZATION/ FORFEITURE	RESTRICTED PLATES FOR PRIVILEGES
	If under 18* If over 18 but under 21**	If over 18 see N. 1 If under 18 see N. 2	No	No

Kentucky DOSI / DUI KRS 189A.090

Operating motor vehicle while license is revoked or suspended for driving under the influence/driving without required ignition interlock

NUMBER OF OFFENSE	DEGREE OF OFFENSE	INCARCERATION	FINES	TREATMENT	
1ST IN 5 YEARS	Class B Misdemeanor	0-90 days	Up to $250	None	
1ST WITH AGGRAVATOR IN 5 YEARS	Class A Misdemeanor	Up to 1 year	Up to $500	For DUI	
2ND IN 5 YEARS	Class A Misdemeanor	Up to 1 year	Up to $500	None	
2ND WITH AGGRAVATOR IN 5 YEARS	Class D Felony	1-5 years	$1,000-$10,000	For DUI	
3RD OR MORE IN 5 YEARS	Class D Felony	1-5 years	$1,000-$10,000	None	
3RD OR MORE WITH AGGRAVATOR IN 5 YEARS	Class D Felony	1-5 years	$1,000-$10,000	For DUI	

	MANDATORY LICENSE SUSPENSION	DRIVING PRIVILEGES	IMMOBILIZATION/ FORFEITURE	RESTRICTED PLATES FOR PRIVILEGES
	6 months	None	None	None
	1 year	None	None	None
	1 year	None	None	None
	2 years	None	None	None
	2 years	None	None	None
	5 years	None	None	None

Not Guilty Adams Contact Information

THE LAW OFFICES OF STEVEN R. ADAMS hopes that this book and the DUI Blackjack strategy are a valuable and informative resource on the issues of DUI/OVI in Ohio and Kentucky. If you, a loved one, or a friend is facing an OVI or DUI, it is critical that you have knowledgeable and experienced counsel on your side. At The Law Offices of Steven R. Adams, we have the lawyers that you need in order to fight for you and protect your rights.

Do not hesitate to contact us at 513-929-9333 or email at STEVEN@NOTGUILTYADAMS.COM.

Also, for further information go to WWW.NOTGUILTYADAMS.COM.

About the Author

STEVEN R. ADAMS began his legal career by clerking for Judge Norbert A. Nadel in a busy, bustling Cincinnati courtroom. He intently studied everything that happened both inside and outside Chambers to better understand how the judge processed information and made decisions. He was also able to watch dozens of trials to identify themes in how jurors behave and reacted to types of evidence, judges, and different styles of attorneys. Mr. Adams spent nearly a decade as an assistant Hamilton County prosecuting attorney. In this position, he successfully prosecuted crimes of all types, from traffic tickets to DUI to murder. He practiced and sharpened his skills with over 1000 trials, both jury and bench. In 2001, Mr. Adams took this vast experience he had accumulated by working in the courtroom and for the prosecution and founded The Law Offices of Steven R. Adams. In his firm, Mr. Adams and his lawyers concentrate on criminal defense and OVI/DUI defense. The firm became, and remains, a premier criminal defense firm using Mr. Adams's background and knowledge to provide client with superior representation. Building on his success, Mr. Adams continues to defend and win cases in the states he has chosen to focus. He is licensed to practice law in Ohio, Kentucky, and the United States District Court for the Southern District of Ohio.

In his never-ending quest to defend his clients, Mr. Adams expanded his DUI education by meticulously researching and studying the law, standardized field sobriety testing, and chemical testing. He believes that the best way to challenge an expert is to know more than the police officer and state expert. To this end, he obtained the necessary training and became qualified to administer standardized field sobriety test (SFSTs) under the National Highway Traffic Safety Administration (NHTSA), and the International Association of Chiefs of Police (IACP) guidelines. Mr. Adams went on to complete training for instructors and successfully completed NHTA's DWI detection and standardized field sobriety testing instructor development training program. Additionally, he trained and became able to operate all three breath testing machines used in Ohio (Intoxilyzer 5000 and 8000 as well as the BAC Data Master). Mr. Adams has consulted on dozens of cases as it relates to serving as an expert witness in SFST's and breath testing. Mr. Adams has been qualified by Ohio courts as an expert on both standardized field sobriety testing and breath testing; he has been sought to provide testimony on both subjects. His status as an expert has been mentioned in State v. Ott (SFST's) and State v. Fischer (breath testing).

Mr. Adams' record is proof of his commitment and dedication to his legal career and his clients. He has had numerous favorable outcomes and decisions in litigating criminal cases and DUI cases, including but not limited to jury trials, bench trials, motions to suppress, and/or pretrial motions throughout the course of his career as a defense attorney. He has served as lead counsel in numerous favorable appellate decisions in Ohio. Mr. Adams has twice argued before the Ohio Supreme Court as Chief Counsel. He was first chair on State v. Ilg a seminal case in which the Ohio Supreme Court agreed with Mr. Adams by holding that an accused can challenge the reliability of breath test results. This decision had a major impact in changing the entire landscape of defense attorneys challenging chemical tests in OVI cases in Ohio.

Mr. Adams' knowledge and skill is well known and he is frequently sought out by both regional and national media outlets to discuss DUI and criminal related topics. He has appeared on several radio shows and television news stations, including Hannity and Colmes (on Fox News Channel) and the Situation Room with Wolf Blitzer. In addition, he has been interviewed by the Cincinnati Enquirer and Columbus Dispatch. His work has also been mentioned in the Chicago Tribune.

Mr. Adams is co-author of ***OHIO OVI DEFENSE: THE LAW AND PRACTICE, KENTUCKY DUI DEFENSE: THE LAW AND PRACTICE*** and Amazon best-selling author of ***PRACTICE LAW LIKE AN IRONMAN***.

Mr. Adams lives in Cincinnati, Ohio with his wife and two sons. His interests are traveling, exercise, fine wines and great craft beers. His high-energy career is matched by his high-energy lifestyle. Four times he has qualified and competed in the Ironman Triathlon World Championships in Hawaii. In three of those four World Championships, he finished the competition as the number one lawyer in the world. Humorous and educational is how Mr. Adams is seen by his colleagues and clients; this is evident in his informative videos on **HTTP://WWW.NOTGUILTYADAMS.COM.** Check it out!

Accolades for Steven R. Adams

STEVEN R. ADAMS RECEIVES SUPERB AVVO RATING 2016–2020

Steve Adams is one of a select group of attorneys who has received a rating of **"SUPERB" FROM AVVO.COM** (a website that contains reviews and helpful information about lawyers in your area). This prestigious distinction is given to attorneys who are top-notch performers in their industry and who have been rated well amongst their clients and peers.

STEVEN R. ADAMS SELECTED FOR BEST LAWYERS IN AMERICA

2016–2020. Congratulations to Steven R. Adams who has been selected by his peers for inclusion in **THE BEST LAWYERS IN AMERICA** for his work in Criminal Defense: General Practice, and DUI/DWI Defense. Recognition by Best Lawyers is based entirely on peer review. Best Lawyers employs a sophisticated, conscientious, rational, and transparent survey process designed to elicit meaningful and substantive evaluations of the quality of legal services.

Best Lawyers® compiles its list of outstanding attorneys through tens of thousands of confidential peer-review surveys. Lawyers are nominated solely based on their professional accomplishments and contributions to the legal field, and cannot nominate themselves or pay to be included in the list. The 2016 edition of Best Lawyers in America includes more than 55,000 lawyers in 140 areas of practice, and was compiled based on more than 6.7 million peer-review surveys. To be included in this list is a huge accomplishment that truly speaks to Attorney Adams' outstanding skill and reputation in Ohio and throughout the country.

In addition to inclusion in Best Lawyers, Attorney Adams has also been named to the prestigious list of **OHIO SUPER LAWYERS®** and has earned an **AV® PREEMINENT™ RATING FROM MARTINDALE-HUBBELL®**. As a result of the efforts of Attorney Adams, The Law Offices of Steven R. Adams, LLC has grown to be recognized as one of the most distinguished law firms in Ohio.

STEVEN R. ADAMS: OHIO SUPER LAWYER 10 YEARS IN A ROW

THE OHIO SUPER LAWYERS 2020 LIST is out and we are honored to have Steven R. Adams as one of Ohio's Super Lawyers for the **10TH YEAR IN A ROW**. Super Lawyers is a rating service of outstanding lawyers from more than 70 practice areas who have gained a high-degree of peer recognition and professional achievement.

WA